This book belongs to

I AM CURIOUS! WHO CREATED US?

Zabed Mohammad, PhD.
Educator & Researcher
Canada

Edited by
Muhammad Zohurul Islam

Published by

Kids Edu Care

Library of Congress Cataloging-in-Publication Data
ISBN: 978-1-998923-09-0

Publisher
Kids Edu Care Inc.
Children's Dedicated Learning Series
Website: www.kidseducare.ca
Illustration Copyright © 2022 by
Kids Edu Care Inc.
Canada

Illustration & Design
Bee Digital

beedigital.asia

info@beedigital.asia

Hmm. I am curious! Who created me?

It is interesting; I am curious, too!

I am curious!
When I was a baby,
how did I cry and smile?

Wow, I am curious to know, too!
Was this my parents, or...

I am curious! from being a new born baby,
how did I grow up?

I am also curious. Was this my parents,
or someone else?

I am curious! While I was still a baby,
I started to see my mom and
my surroundings by
using my eyes.
Who gave me two eyes to see?

Yes, I am curious, too.
Is this a gift from my parents,
or someone else?

I am curious! While I was a baby,
how did I know to breathe in and out?
Who gave me that ability?

I am curious, too.
I am also wondering
if this is from my parents.

I am curious! While I was a baby,
who arranged the milk for
me from my mom's breast?

Yes, I am also curious to know.
Is this from my mom, or from someone else?

I am curious! While I was a baby,
I was not able to talk,
but now I can.
Who gave me this ability?

Yes, I am also curious.
Is this gift from my parents,
or from someone else?

I am curious!
Even while I was a baby,
I could hear sounds.
Who gave me two ears to hear?

Yes, I'm curious, too.
Is this from my parents, or someone else?

I am curious! While I was a baby,
I had no teeth.
But now I do,
and I can eat what I like.

Yes, I am also curious.
Is this a gift from my parents,
or from someone else?

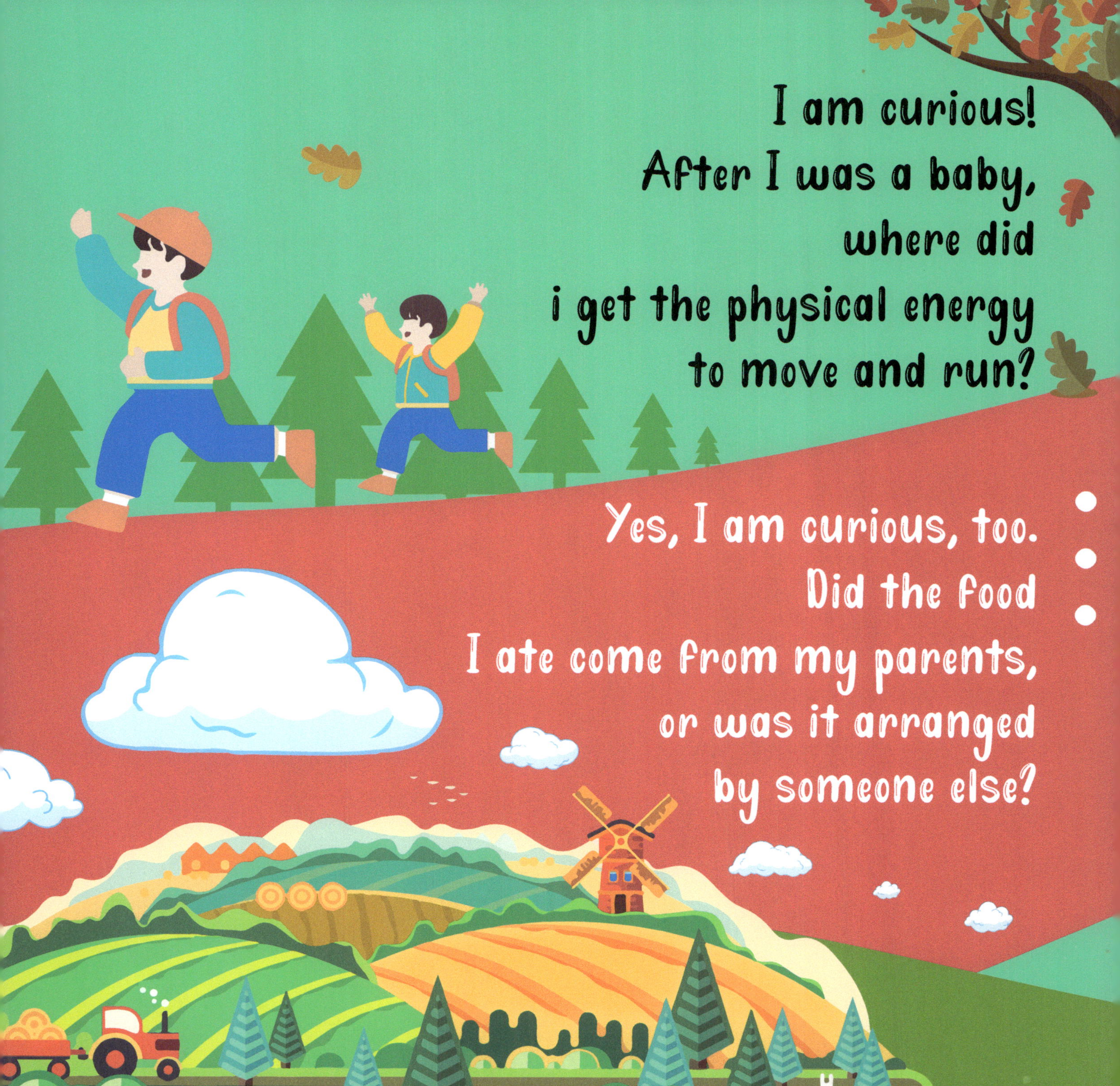

I am curious!
After I was a baby,
where did
i get the physical energy
to move and run?

Yes, I am curious, too.
Did the food
I ate come from my parents,
or was it arranged
by someone else?

I am curious!
While I was a baby,
where did I get the ability to think?

Yes, I am also curious to know.
Is this a gift from my parents
or from someone else?

I am curious! When I was born,
who gave me two hands
and ten fingers to touch and hold things?

Yes, I'm also curious.
Is this a gift from my parents,
or from someone else?

I am curious!
When I was a baby,
I was not able to walk,
run, or jump.
But now I can.
who gave me this strength?

Yes, I am also curious to know.
Is this a gift from my parents, or....

I am curious! While I was a baby,
I had to wear diapers,
and was not able to use the washroom.
But now I can. Who gave me this ability?

Yes, I am also curious.
Where did this ability come from?

I am curious! While I was a baby,
How I recognize my parents
who are they?
Is there anyone who gave me
this recognizing ability?

Yes, I am also curious
to know. Did this ability come from
my parents, or from somewhere?

I am curious!
While I was a baby,
I was not able to
understand how to behave
with elders, parents and so on.
But now I know how I should behave.
Who gave me this understanding ability?

Yes, I am also curious to know.
Did this ability come from my parents,
or from someone else?

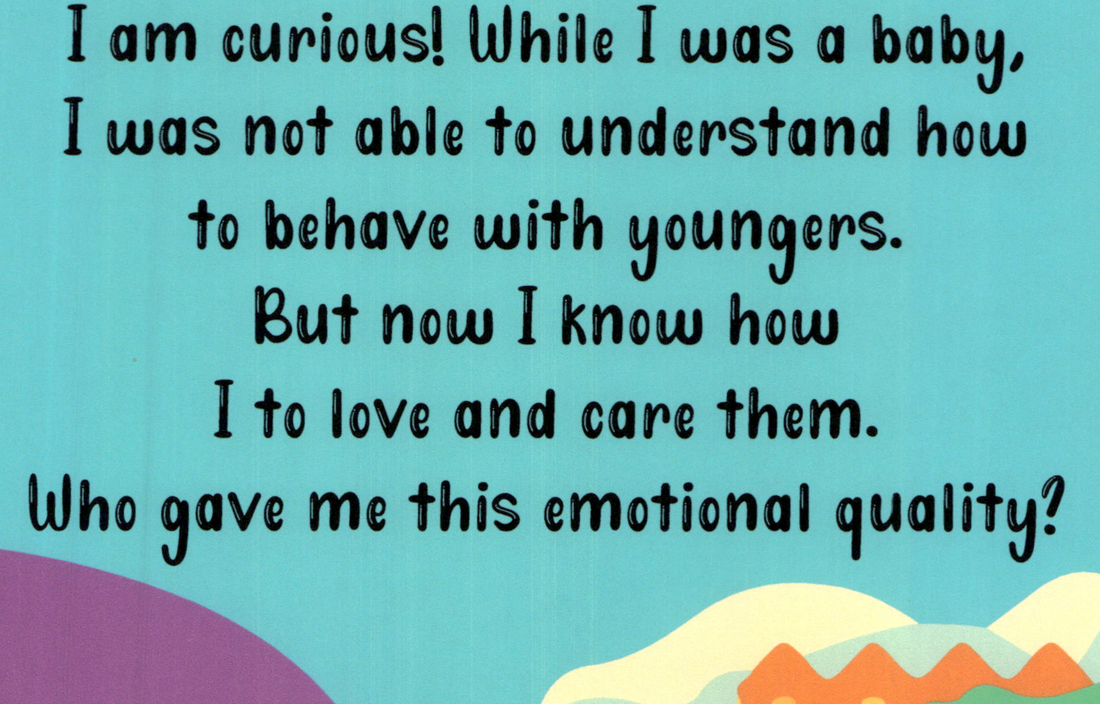

I am curious! While I was a baby,
I was not able to understand how
to behave with youngers.
But now I know how
I to love and care them.
Who gave me this emotional quality?

Yes, I also wonder about this.
Is this knowledge a gift from
my parents, or from
someone else?

I am curious! While I was a baby,
I was not able to read and write.
But now I can.
Who gave me that
reading and writing ability?

Yes, I am also curious to know,
is this my school teacher
gift me like something else?

I am curious! While I was baby,
who gave me healthy brain
and nice physical conditions?

Yes, I am curious too.

I am curious!
While I was a baby,
I was solely dependent on my parents,
and was unable to make a decision
or perform any task!

Wow! Now a days
I can think
and take the decision
to be forward...

I am curious! While I was a baby,
I was solely dependent on my parents,
and was unable to do
whatI can do today! Why is that?

Hmm, I agree.
That is why I think about
whom we should be grateful to!

All these developments and improvements come from the bounty of our Creator. Therefore, all success also comes from our Creator, so I must be grateful to Allah (SWT).

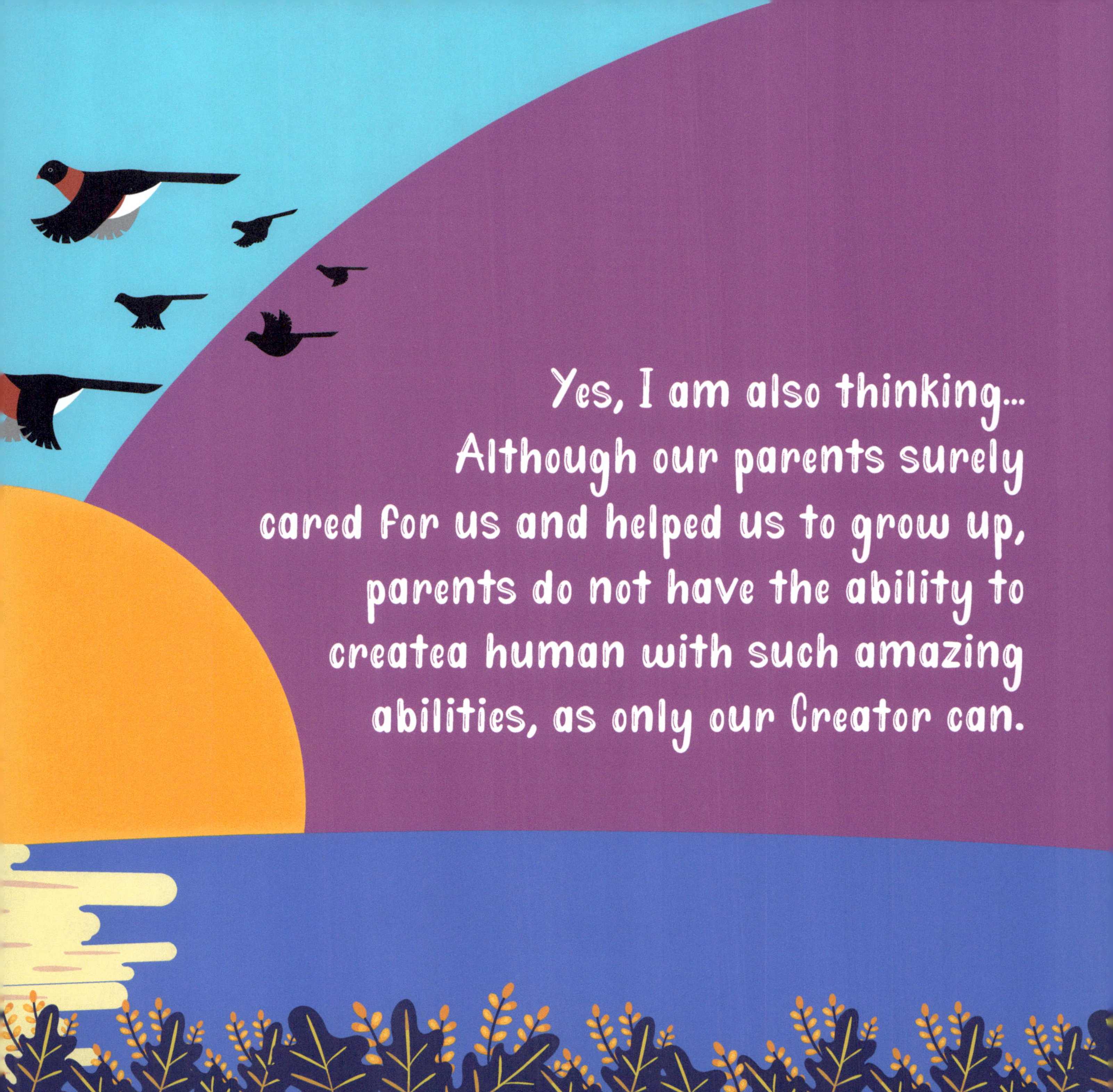

Yes, I am also thinking...
Although our parents surely
cared for us and helped us to grow up,
parents do not have the ability to
createa human with such amazing
abilities, as only our Creator can.

So, I am grateful to our Creator
for giving me all my wonderful
abilities and strengths.

Other great books by Zabed Mohammad!

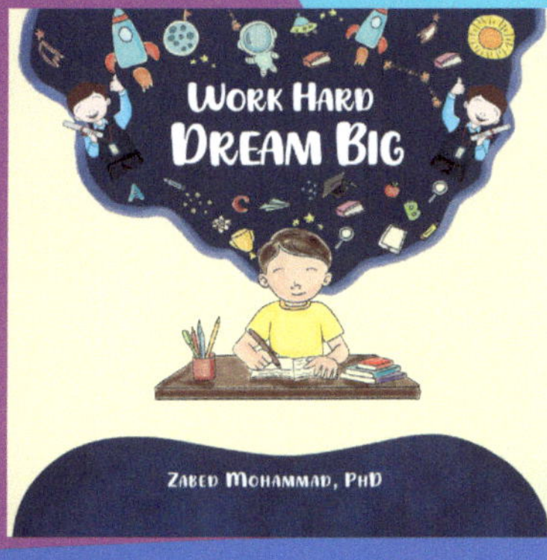

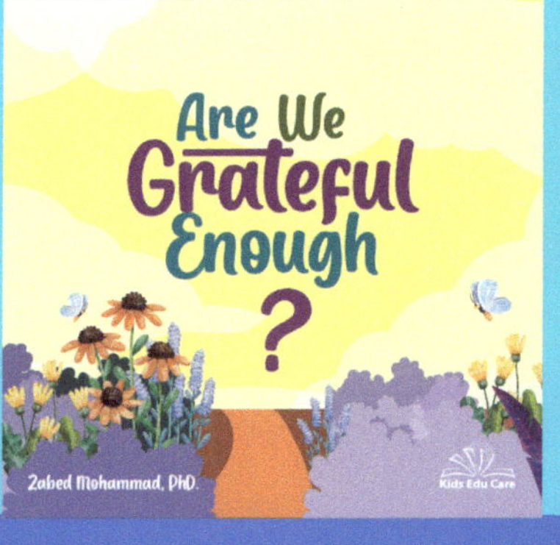

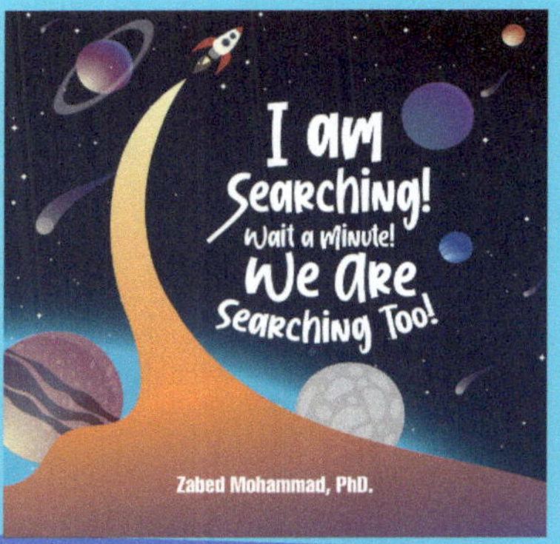

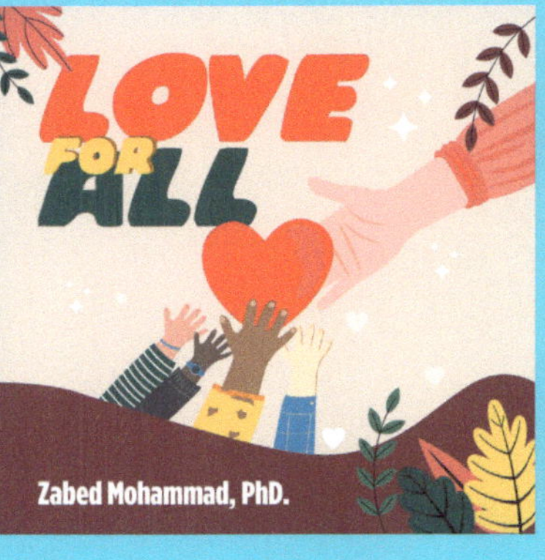

We hope you may like them!